We Give Birth to Light

poems by

Benjamin D. Carson

Finishing Line Press
Georgetown, Kentucky

We Give Birth to Light

ACKNOWLEDGMENTS

"What It Cost Us," "Black Hole Moon," "Lordan Road," and "We Give Birth
to Light" in *Eunoia Review*
"We Give Birth to Light" on poet Doug Holder's Boston Area Small Press
and Poetry Scene blog
"Unforgiven" in *Rumble Fish Quarterly*
"Halos" and "After Whiskey" in *Right Hand Pointing*
"The Poetry of My Final Days" as "For W.S. Merwin" in *The Poetry Porch*
"Beach Stones" in *Gyroscope*
"Staring into the Sun" and "This Is Just How It Is" in *Oddball Magazine*
"Waiting for the Stars to Fall" in *Dunes Review*
"The Last E Train to Far Rockaway" in *BOOG City*
"Breakfast at the Diner, Christmas Eve" in *Poetry Leaves*
"The Bookish Light" in *Crosswinds*
"The Numbing Drift" in *Toho Journal*
"The Healing Ground" in *South Dakota in Poems*, South Dakota State Poetry
Society, ed. Christine Stewart-Nuñez (Poet Laureate of South Dakota)
"For a Time" in *Blood and Thunder: Musings on the Art of Medicine*,
Oklahoma University College of Medicine
"The Way It Is or Isn't" in *Monday Night*; republished in *Color:Story*
alongside original artwork, inspired by the poem, by Leslie Gaworecki

Publisher: Leah Huete de Maines
Editor: Christen Kincaid
Cover Art: Benjamin D. Carson, "Sunrise over Project Somos, Tecpan,
        Guatemala"
Author Photo: Janene Johnson
Cover Design: Elizabeth Maines McCleavy

Order online: www.finishinglinepress.com
        also available on amazon.com

Author inquiries and mail orders:
Finishing Line Press
PO Box 1626
Georgetown, Kentucky 40324
USA

Table of Contents

To my
Mother and Father

The Way It Is or Isn't

I prefer to rise with the sun
and swim in my neighbor's pond.
I prefer to take tea in the morning
and again in the afternoon.
I prefer to raise wild orchids
and cut my corn off the cob.
I prefer the sound of rain to thunder
and autumn and winter and
spring and summer to their end.
I prefer reading by candlelight
and running by the light of the moon.

These things I prefer but do not demand.
There are whole days without tea.
Some seasons the orchids wilt
and I must use my teeth on the cob.
Sometimes the pond is frozen over,
and there is thunder but little rain.
Some nights the clouds hide the moon
and autumn and winter and spring
and summer seem each to live forever.
But that is ok by me. I prefer it this way,
the way it is or isn't. All of it is preferable
as it is. There is nothing I'd have otherwise.

This Is Just How It Is

On a farm in Iowa, during the Second Great War,
my mother made dresses out of parachutes. She
lost her teeth playing "crack the whip," raised
goats and cut heads off of chickens. On the night
she died, she said, quietly, through a toothless grin,
"This is just how the world is. This is just how it is.
Goats. Chickens. And dancing like we're falling
from the sky."

Staring into the Sun

My grandmother smiled through milky eyes.
I watched, as smoke spiraled out from her cigarette,
held by a gnarled hand, her wheelchair pushed back
against the wall. "I've seen it all," she said, "stared
right at it. Nothing wasn't worth looking at, nothing
worth ignoring." She pointed to the ceiling, water-stained
and peeling, a tapestry of neglect. I took a deep breath,
and closed my eyes. "Look for me now. Can you see the
stars? The Seven Sisters. Orion. The Pleiades? I've seen
it all," she said, and laughed. "To see it all is like staring
into the sun, magic until darkness falls."

Waiting for the Stars to Fall

My older brother folded my last dollar bill into a tiny airplane
on the night we sat on the roof waiting for the stars to fall.
A great in-suck of breath shook me as the little fighter drifted
over the edge of the building, taking what little hope I had with it.
María Estela said "Cup-O-Gold is the only way to a girl's heart"
with the kind of sing-song seriousness only a heart-sick boy of nine
could believe, and I knew then that, for me, love was dead.
"Looks like no stars are falling tonight," my brother said
to the vastness of space, his head tipped back, like it was
swinging from a noose. "Looks like no stars are falling tonight,"
he repeated, as the wind caught the wings of that little green bird
and lifted it past the A&P, Dick's Diner, the Post Office,
and the butcher's, and then, just as it rose, as if to go into orbit,
a currency of dreams, it dove into the creek that runs past the mill,
a vein of running darkness sprinkled with light.

Halos

My father's body rests on the hill,
my mother's underground,
two long shadows. Late Day.
To the sound of swallows, I rise to go,
as sun dogs hang and blaze
linear tombs of light.

The Bookish Light

We were reading Strand's "Eating Poetry," and the kid
with the baseball hat and sad eyes said the poem makes
him hungry, and the girl who is always late and is never
without gum said she is afraid of dogs, which is mainly
why she doesn't like *like* the poem or something.

When I suggest we take a close look at the line "the dogs are
on the basement stairs and coming up," their eyeballs roll,
and for an unbelieving moment I think they are with me.
Suzie, who always sits in the front row, her hands buried
in the folds of her dress, looks like she is going to cry. Mona,
who means well, tells me her mother is a librarian and would
never allow dogs in the building.

I am an old man, I think, tugging at my collar, too old to bark,
too old to snarl. So I say, let us begin at the beginning, and I
begin to read, and at "the poor librarian begins to stamp her
feet and weep," I close my eyes and go on, the lines lifting me
up and joyously away, toward the bookish light.

Unforgiven

*"Close pent-up guilts /
Rive your concealing continents and cry /
These dreadful summoners grace."* —King Lear

In the picture my grandmother held of my grandfather,
he sat astride a young gelding, a gift, she smiled, for his
fortieth birthday. "The bastard stood fourteen hands," she
said, and I wasn't sure if she was talking about the horse
or the man, who, in the picture, was straight-backed, a
little wild-eyed, which over the years was tamed out of him,
as if he'd been ridden hard, corralled against his will, and finally
tethered to a stake, and, as family lore has it, it was my grand-
mother who broke him, the man she hadn't seen in twenty-
five years.

On the back of the picture, left on the table the night he dis-
appeared, one word was written in my grandfather's galloping
scrawl: Unforgiven. And, for my grandmother, it was all she
needed to know she'd taken it too far, that his need to run was
in his blood, and was as harmless as a cockle-bur hitching it on
the gelding's cresty mane. The horse wasn't just a gift; it was her
way of telling her man it was time to come in "out of the heat,"
she said, as if I knew what that meant. I was nine at the time, and
she was eighty-five, gray-eyed, gray-haired, with thick calloused
hands, as though she'd been holding a rope for decades.

"I took it too far," she said, setting the picture on the table, and
hugging me into her chest, as she began to recount the way my
grandfather made her coffee each morning, a cup three-quarters
full and a tab of saccharine; how he'd take in the laundry after a hot
day in the field, making sure to wash his hands before folding the
sheets; how he praised her cooking, her soggy vegetables and bone
dry chicken; and how he, on cold winter nights, put extra blankets on
the bed, kissed her forehead, and wrapped his body around hers to
keep her shivering teeth from rattling out of her head—and at the
memories, her voice caught in her throat.

Then, as I slid off her thighs, she slumped in her chair. "I took it too far," she repeated. "I never let him forget that he used to love to roam, though the hills he loved weren't of the breedin' kind but the contours of his very life. And then he rode off." On the night of his sixtieth birthday, my grandfather guided the gelding out of the barn, saddled him, mounted up, and headed south. No one knows this for sure, because no one saw him go, and no one has seen him since. Even now, twenty years on, when I can't sleep, I can still see an old man gliding across the plains on a horse, a lone rider, the ghost of a man who, once wild, sought grace in gestures, and got only silence until home wasn't home any more.

The Healing Ground
(for Mary Icayapawin)

She lived and died on the Saw Kill, the old woman
sewing nets and selling worms to anglers like my
father, who came up from the city, stayed in her barn
and swore by her dry flies and her medicine.

The year I turned eleven, the year my mother died, my
father took me to the kill; the woods through which it
cut were where the old woman found her Box Elder and
Redbud bark, blackberry roots, and prickly pear.

My father told me she cured sore throats with the boiled
nest of a mud dauber, toothaches with bean tree bark, and
pimples with mule tail weed, snake bites with a poultice of
mud and clay.

She had the power to heal, he said in the silence that weighed
down the night, the air in the barn loft thick with what neither
of us could say. Tomorrow we'd try our flies and our luck on
the Saw Kill, on the seam that cuts through the healing ground,
where all but one cure could be found.

Prompt

I asked my ex- for a prompt, she gave me gasoline; she said
you're the poet, light your own damn fire, set ablaze your
own regrets, your own past. Stack them all up in a word-pyre,
brittle and dry, and light a match; let the smoke settle deep
in your lungs and sting your eyes and yellow your skin. Let
the flames lick at all that you were before you turn to ash.

The Last E Train to Far Rockaway

I just made the last E Train to Far Rockaway.
My head splitting, my stomach a cauldron, my breath
a sinister mix of cheeseburger and kerosene. One of
three bodies in the car, I slumped into a seat as it
rolled out of the station. A grey-haired old man
in a long grey coat read a newspaper. Looked like
he wasn't wearing any pants. Black socks sunk into
loafers. Hairy skin sagged on bone. His lips moved,
as though he were reading aloud, or chanting to the
clash and clank of the swaying train.
       And there she was,
sleeping fitfully, curled up into a ball, her oil stained
jeans tucked into her socks, her Keds untied, the laces
draped over the seat like icicles, her hair dripping
down like dirty tears. When she yawned, I could see
her shirt said, YOUR LOGO HERE, and I moved
closer, pulled inexorably by the need to name her, and
then to name him. To name this moment, a triptych of
blank canvases—him, her, me.
       Nothing. Not gold.
Not frankincense. No star heralding our arrival. Just
myrrh, I thought, as the man coughed in his sleep, the
newspaper now blanketing his legs. And then, from
some deep reservoir, the girl hissed, "Thisss is sweeeeter
than wine." And, from her mouth, the faintest whiff of
alcohol seemed to propel the train, this roaring snake,
deeper and deeper into the tunnel, and farther and
farther into the hard and awful night.

After Whiskey

After whiskey, everything turns.
The breeze through the window
is the very breath of life, and the
moon is the only light there is.
What should be remembered
is forgotten, and what is forgotten
rears its head. It's not alchemy.
There's nothing magic about this.
It's whiskey, which sits in the back
of your throat like smoke and turns
the spirit to fire.

The Stain

I knew from the stain in
the crotch of her panties
what we had lost, and
felt in my chest the
nothing we had gained.

Beach Stones

We've been rubbing up against each other for so long we've worn all of our edges off, those sharp angles, the little divots and nooks that make you you and me me. It must have been the waves pulling us in and out, back and forth with the tide, led by the force of the moon, that has left us so smooth.

And now, as I have grown round, and you have grown round, too, we can no longer sink into one another when the salt water washes over us. I always knew you were stone, but your hardness surprises me, even as now I have nothing to reach for, and nothing to receive me.

Surface of Last Scattering

She said we've reached our limit,
the outermost edge of our little,
untidy universe. It is time to go.
But there are no edges, I said,
nowhere to go, which is why
we just go round and round and
round, circling this endless space,
always back where we started,
slipping and sliding across this
surface of last scattering.

The Cave and the Light

My wisdom teeth lay flat in the back of my mouth,
inaccessible, deep against bone and nerve. Taking
them out is too dangerous, I'm told. I could be left
without feeling where there was never any pain until
those teeth were extricated, brought out of the cave
of my mouth, and into the light.

Black Hole Moon

I caught a three-pound musky on the night
a bag of puppies was tossed off a bridge
into the Susquehanna. As the little wriggling
sack of cries and yips bobbed in the current,
two and then four and then six little stars
emerged in a whirlpool of foam and darkness,
and then, one by one, the lights went out. In
the silence that followed, I slid the fish off the
stringer and, by the glow of the moon, watched
it drift and then, as if by the tug of a leash,
disappear into the shadows of the living and
the ghosts of the dead.

The Numbing Drift

I wonder what he was thinking the last time he dove into that river headfirst like a bombardier, a kamikaze, a spirit wind, the tip of a spear. Launching himself off of that boat, the sun hot on his wide and strong shoulders, was it joy he felt? As he sailed through the air, arms stiff to his sides, was he smiling, anticipating the coolness of the water, the tug of the current, as it pulled at his chest, enveloped his thighs and feet?

What was it he thought as his head hit the sandbar hiding just beneath the silt and the waves, as his neck twisted obscenely, backward and up, his distorted smile now buried under the weight of his body as it drove his head down and down and down and into the grit? What must it be like, that first moment of unfeeling?

How light, I wonder, must be this numbing drift, the sense that life is just barely the weight of thought, a head perched on a mountain of flesh, floating unmoved, hearing, seeing, and knowing that what nourishes it now comes through the tip of a straw.

Lordan Road

At the end of Lordan Road, I see a man standing at the edge of a pond, his boots tucked into his jeans, his hands stuffed into his coat; a cap covers the tips of his ears. In the last hours of the day, he, in his stillness, could be mistaken for a statue or a tree. His only companion, a fishing rod, like a single, thirsty limb, reaches out over the water; a thread, like a silver tongue, hanging from its tip, disappears into the darkening pool. It is the end of the line.

What It Cost Us

We were so high that summer for which we all now atone,
the summer T blew his brains out and S's body was dumped,
dead, in a ditch across from a golf course; the summer R put
a chair through every window in our apartment, holes in one;
the summer J got married to a woman who would shortly die,
her breasts eaten away from cancer; the summer K slept with A
who was loved by R who slept with N who fucked, despite her
beauty, like a corpse; the summer I found in my bed one stoned
night a woman from whom I'd later move to France to escape—
the consequence of *la petite mort*. It was the summer we all died a
little, so high we couldn't see ourselves, earthbound and mortal;
we couldn't see ourselves and what, in years of wonder and regret,
it would cost.

Breakfast at the Diner, Christmas Eve

The old man orders corned beef hash, his wife Eggs Benedict.
"I can't eat," she whispers, poking at her food. He nods. "Try
a bite, baby. Just one." "Maybe," she says, tapping her fork
to Christmas Muzak. He eats and watches her, his face sagging
in worry. She's been tired lately, he thinks. Too tired. As she
turns to look out the window, he can see her skull through her
thinning hair, the dark circles under her eyes.

"It's back," she says softly. And looking down at his plate, he says
almost inaudibly, "I know." "It's here!" she says with enough life to
startle him, and he follows her eyes outside. Flakes, like cotton, fall
from the sky, drifting in the icy air. "It always comes back, doesn't it?
And . . . it's always a kind of miracle," she says, and when she reaches
out her hand, as if to catch the coming storm in her palm, his is there
to meet it.

For a Time
(for Tony Hoagland)

For a time I thought I knew what it meant to die slowly.
I'd been watching my wife's body eat itself for months.

In the first days after the doctor told her she had very
little time, she walked among us as she always had, her

shoulders back, her head always tilting a little to the left,
as though struggling to form a stubborn thought that she

needed to get out, her most innocuous statements ending
with a lilt that suggested a question. This is how we knew

her, how our boys saw her, the way they saw long Sunday
afternoons and hot summer days, just the rhythm of a life

that always was and, for all they knew, would always be.
If this was dying, it looks a lot like living, I thought in those

early days, days when I went to work like I always did—after
a cup of coffee and a kiss, Marie standing on the front step

with the newspaper tucked under her arm and waving. For a
time, whatever fear we felt, hardly in equal measure, was

defended against by routine: brushing teeth; washing clothes;
doing homework; cutting the grass; tuning in to our favorite

shows—mom, dad, kids in a heap on the couch, a family impregnable.
And then she began to cough, and then she began to bleed, and

nothing would stay down, her vomit a thin gruel of bile and blood.
The only thing with an appetite was inside her and binging on her

liver, her kidneys, her lungs, the lining of her stomach, which she
used to brag was made of iron. A week of this, two weeks, and

then a month, two months, and then, the end, the blessed final
retch, the silent scream that bent her in half, followed by a silence

that I can still hear, and feel, this scene, an ancient tableau, as old
as bone and the dust from which it came, a moment framed not just

for a time, but forever.

The Coming Days without Her
(for ARW)

The days without her come,
and I'm surprised by that, honestly.
I wake to darkness, my chest weighed down
with sadness rocks, cairns that point,
by the light of the quarter moon,
a wolf's eye, to what I imagine are
canyons, arroyos of grief.
I hear the morning, a snarl, say,
Come. Get up. It's here.
But I say no, not another day without her.
And the day says, there are no other days.
This is it. Howl.

The Poetry of My Final Days
(for Donald Hall)

*"How did I come to this late happiness /
as I wake into my remaining days"* —W.S. Merwin

There seems now nothing left to be tired of. This age
that has come upon me like a thunderstorm rolling
across the plains has left in its wake an ache in my
bones and a longing for something I can no longer
name, which may just be what longing is, a nameless
something that is a nothing that is nonetheless there.
I didn't think it'd quite be like this, a time when
what was is greater than what will be, a past that is
truly past. I don't, like the poet I most admire, wake
to a late happiness, but rather the tug of a thread that
is strong enough to suggest rising but thin enough
to threaten its opposite, in perpetuity, the body supine,
eyes skyward. No. I'm not waiting for death. I'm not
really waiting for anything, just aching and longing—
two words that have become the poetry of my final days.

Last Walk

The rain had just stopped, and what looked like an
old rainbow muscled its way through the blue sky.
No one will believe me, I thought. It's too poetic,
too perfect. This was Dora's last walk, though it was
not really a walk. She mostly just stood by the side of
the road, smelling the wet grass, the cool air. Age had
finally caught up with her, and there was only one place
left to go. She teetered a little as she looked down the
road she'd walked almost daily for fourteen years, a last
look at the horizon she could no longer see, her eyes
now as gray as her once white snout. She turned to look
at me, as though to tell me it was time. The rainbow gone,
we turned back to the house and slowly towards the car.
Soon it would be noon, and then night.

We Give Birth to Light

The moon rose full over the cemetery
on the night my mother gave birth to her son,
his face round, his lips blue. This will be
the last one, she said. There will be no more.

The sun set an autumn orange over the field
on the night my mother watched my father take to the road,
his face chapped, his hands raw. This will be
the last harvest, she said. There won't be another.

The North Star, my mother once said to no one, is the only
light that matters, the one that shines and shines
and shines, even after the last breath is taken,
the field abandoned, the lover lost.

We give birth to light, she muttered, so that
darkness too can have its day.

Additional Acknowledgments

For their encouragement, inspiration, and forbearance, often in equal measure, I'd like to thank:

Lori LeComte, Rob Radack, Joshua Doležal, Tonya Moutray, Andrea Julie Kamins, Sonja Saunders, Antje Duvekot, John Mulrooney, Abigail Wotton, Takako Johnson, and Robert, Kellie, and Sarah Carson.

I would like to express my gratitude to the men, my brothers, at Old Colony Correctional Complex—may the light in me honor the light in you.

A special thank you to Ted Richer, poet, mentor, friend.

This book is dedicated to my late father, Clarence (Bud) Nolan Carson, Jr., and my mother, Delora (Dee) Lynn Carson—without whom not.

Benjamin D. Carson is a Professor of English at Bridgewater State University. His creative work has appeared in many literary journals, including *Rumble Fish Quarterly*, *Poetry Porch*, *Dunes Review*, *Yellow Medicine Review*, and *October Hill Magazine*. He lives with his dog Dora in Bridgewater, MA.

CPSIA information can be obtained
at www.ICGtesting.com
Printed in the USA
JSHW022033240521
15153JS00001B/67